WHAT IS STOPPING YOU

HILLARY DUNKLEY-CAMPBELL

Copyright © 2022
HILLARY DUNKLEY CAMPBELL

All rights reserved. No part of this publication may be reproduced, copied, stored in a retrieval system, transmitted, or scanned in any form or under any conditions, including, photocopying, electronic, recording, or otherwise, without the written permission of the author, HILLARY DUNKLEY CAMPBELL.

ISBN: 978-1-954755-27-7

Published by:
Restoration of the Breach without Borders
West Palm Beach, Florida 33407
restorativeauthor@gmail.com
Tele: (475) 233-9008

Unless otherwise stated Scripture verses are quoted from the King James Version of the Bible.

Table of Contents

Dedication	iii
Endorsements	v
Foreword	vii
Introduction	1
What is stopping you?	1
Chapter 1: The Traffic Light	3
Chapter 2: Fear	21
Chapter 3: Doubt	30
Chapter 4: Discouragement	36
Chapter 5: Self-Sabotage	46
Chapter 6: Insecurity	52
Chapter 7: Procrastination	57
Chapter 8: People's Opinion	64
Chapter 9: Worry	72
Chapter 10: Prayer: The Antidote to Worry	80
Chapter 11: Adversity	87
Chapter 12: Sin	98
Chapter 13: Just Do it!	106
Reference	115
About The Author	116

Dedication

I dedicate this book to those who are stuck in a rout and feel like they cannot get going. My prayer is that as you read this book you will become empowered, inspired, hopeful, determined, and encouraged to get going.

Endorsements

I must say congratulations on your book!

This book is a great addition to the body of Christ. It points out the destructive and divisive way in which the enemy tries to derail us from our walking in our God-given purpose. It does this by highlighting the many obstacles that we are faced with constantly daily by giving examples and a game plan. This book seeks to enlighten us in the strategies and the ways we can overcome the wiles of the enemy and battle effectively. The best way to beat the enemy is to know the real enemy and this book definitely does that!

>   -C. R. Laing
>   Senior pastor
>   Victory Family Centre

It is very refreshing to know that there are still people who are focused on finding solutions to life's challenges. Hillary Dunkley is one such person, she has written this book, and it is a must-read. This book allows you to do deep introspection in order to find problems that have been holding you back while motivating and inspiring you to find the great solutions for your success. This book is universal in its outlook as it caters to everyone who wants to be successful. It is essential in that it offers the keys and meaningful principles needed to live a successful life.

I was challenged and reminded while reading it to hold fast to the plans I set out to accomplish. This book will enhance your collection because it's not just for this generation but for generations to come.

-Bishop Davis
Valley Of Light Ministry

Foreword

What is stopping you? Is a very important question that needs to be answered. It's a question that requires some deep introspection and may take some time to answer. In writing this book I encountered challenges that could have stopped me but with the help of the Holy Spirit and my Destiny Helpers you are now holding it in your hands. I submit to you that as you read this book to not just read but make the knowledge given applicable to your life. Stopping should not be an option, giving up should not be considered. God requires you to show up, keep moving and partner with him to complete the good work he has begun in you (Philippians 1:6). There will be times when you need to pause, slow down to regroup and catch your breath.

However, don't get too comfortable in this position, do what is required and keep moving.

>-Hillary Dunkley-Campbell
>Author,
>Introduction
>What is stopping you?

Introduction

What is stopping you?

In life, challenges are inevitable; there is no escaping them. Whether you are rich or poor, black or white, a Christian or non-Christian, you will face setbacks. Challenges however are not always designed to break you; they can be seen as an opportunity to strengthen your faith in the midst of adversity, to build resistance, to gain wisdom and to rely solely on God. You should never allow challenges to stop you from pursuing your purpose, achieving your full potential, or reaching your destiny. There is a popular saying "no pain, no gain." Pain is not welcomed but at times it is necessary. For an amateur boxer to become the heavyweight champion of the world he or she must train hard and be prepared to receive the punches he or she is giving to the opponent in order to win. The truth is, after each fight the boxer's body will ache whether or not he or she wins the fight. As a boxer there is no escape from feeling pain or being hit by the opponent – it comes with the territory. In the same manner, in life you will encounter challenges, disappointments, rejections, oppositions, delays, roadblocks, and the list goes on. However, of paramount importance is the answer to the question; will you allow the mentioned hindrances to stop you? Will you allow your life to be sidelined by negativities? In this book, you will be encouraged and challenged as I address some of the areas that contribute to the main question which is actually the title of this book, "What is stopping you?"

Chapter 1

The Traffic Light

Universally the traffic light has three colors: red, yellow, and green. The green light means go. At the signal of the green light, drivers may turn left, go straight, or turn right after yielding to vehicles and pedestrians already in the intersection. On the other hand, the yellow or amber light means slow down the red light is about to appear therefore you must remain alert and approach with caution. While the red light means you must stop. In the same manner, the traffic light is easily distinguished across the world as a means of maintaining order on the road, God uses His Word, the Holy Spirit, and the challenges of life to keep us in line. In Psalm 32:8 He says: "I will instruct thee and teach thee in the way which thou shalt go I will guide thee with mine eye."

GREENLIGHT

Our lives flow like the traffic. There are some seasons when God says it is time to extend our faith, press gas, and go. In those moments, do not let the negative situations shackle you. Step out in faith start that business, pursue that degree, write that book, or start that relationship. The truth is the green light may come while you are still jammed in the traffic of life, but God is saying stay alert and get ready to take the blessings. When God said to Moses go and deliver the children of Israel they were still stuck in Egypt with a dictator called Pharaoh, Exodus 9:1. In another account, the Jordan River was extremely dirty but Elisha told Naaman go and wash seven times and you shall be clean 2 Kings 5:10. Additionally, the

Jericho walls were still up, they were so thick that two chariots could easily go by without colliding, but Joshua 6:1-2. What is God saying you should go and conquer? Whatever it is, let that be your green light, do not be daunted by the presenting challenges, go in and take the blessings. Yes, you may be in the messiest situation of your life, but your miracle is in your movement. Understand that if you procrastinate in your "go" season the possibility exists that you may miss out on a life changing opportunity. One that might never present itself again. When Abraham was called to leave his homeland, he did not know where he was going but he knew it was the season to move.

By faith Abraham, when he was called to go out into a place which he should after receiving for an inheritance, obeyed; and he went out, not knowing whither he went. (Hebrews 11:8)

Like Abraham you have been called to go- might not be to another country, but probably to a greater dimension at work, study, relationship, or in ministry but you are fearful of the unknown. Take that step. Abraham moved at the green light and that one opportunity saw him becoming the father of many nations. Do not let doubt cripple you to sit through your green light. Your forward movement can be the move that catapults you into your destiny. Abraham was confident that he heard from God and like the drivers in waiting he did not ignore the green light, he and his family quickly moved at God's command. You may not have all the answers but rest in God's security and press the gas pedal of your life.

YELLOW LIGHT

It is important to understand that the "go" season will not last forever. There are times when we are pressing the gas, going after our dreams, and the amber, the yellow light of God's directive appears saying slow down. Like the traffic light, God is not saying come to a halt but stay under the caution light for a while. The appearance of the yellow light does not equate to an immediate stop but requires consciousness that a stop is approaching. It means your go-green season is coming to an end. Amber highlights that the borders of your go season are fast approaching. This means you must now tread cautiously.

However, do not become overly anxious, not just yet. In essence, you are at that place where you need to put off your understanding and seek God for directives. That relationship you are going after, God may be saying go a little slower, it is not an overnight affair, you need to be more prepared, and you need to learn more about your partner. Hence, as you look at God's yellow light it is not time to get distracted, it is just saying refocus. Change your strategy so that you may save the things or people that really matter. Seek wise counsel on the issue. Take some time to breathe. You are so busy going after your dreams that the family, ministry, or even self is being sidelined- slow down. Prioritize, spend time pouring into your loved ones, or even allow others to show their appreciation to you. Most of all recognize that God has just brought you to a place of quiet, trust, and total dependence on Him. Sometimes the slow period can become awkward, you just want to go faster, you are saying you should have achieved that degree already, the business should have been thriving by now, and as such you may be questioning, "When will things change?" "What did I do to be going at snail's pace?" However, God has not brought you to that place to be consumed with doubt but that you can truly reason with Him and find answers that will be clear as day. As you are in your slow period, get deeper into God and His word for that is where you will find all the answers. Psalm 119:105 says, "Thy word is a lamp unto my feet and a light unto my path."

A major error that is made in the yellow light season, is believing that slowdown is all that's available. After the amber/yellow, you will enter into the red zone which is halt/stop. Slowing down too quickly might see you stopping in the wrong dimension. Therefore, a careful evaluation must be quickly executed to determine if this present amber requires slow down or intense acceleration. A careful intense pressing of the gas pedal at the sight of the yellow light can be the difference between the continuing or ending of your green go season.

Miscalculation of the amber can mean

- Prosperity delayed
- Victory Denied
- Accident
- Penalty

RED LIGHT

It is well known that the red light means stop. While going through the stop season, there are a lot of uncertainties. At times you may feel as though you are being punished by God. However, He knows the importance of the stop sign and the wealth the said season will bring to your life. In the book of Matthew, the disciples were revved up; it was all systems go as Jesus said to them:

"Go ye therefore, and teach all nations, baptizing them in the name of the Father, and of the Son, and of the Holy Ghost: Teaching them to observe all things whatsoever I have commanded you: and, lo, I am with you always, even unto the end of the world. Amen." (Matthew 28:19-20).

However, as soon as they were getting excited to go, Jesus said tarry at Jerusalem.

And, being assembled together with them, commanded them that they should not depart from Jerusalem, but wait for the promise of the Father, which, saith he, ye have heard of me (Acts 1:14).

I must say to the natural man that must not have made much sense, and sometimes God telling you to stop cannot be explained. However, Jesus knew the disciples needed the empowerment of the Holy Spirit in order to carry out the Great Commission and same only came after they waited in Jerusalem. The truth is nobody wants to experience a red light but God being Omniscient knows that said light is what will adequately prepare us for our next. Isaiah 55:8-9 says:

For my thoughts are not your thoughts, neither are your ways my ways, saith the LORD. For as the heavens are higher than the earth, so are my ways higher than your ways, and my thoughts than your thoughts.

You may not understand the reason the sickness has come, and the doctors may not be able to explain either, but God will work it for your good. On the other hand, the family is doing well, you are finally able to go on vacation and do the monthly shopping as desired then the news comes- the main breadwinner has lost his/her job. Imagine the disappointment. The family now has to put many things on pause. However, in the midst of all the innumerable circumstances that you see as red light, you still have a choice. Will you allow the things that seem messy to rob you of your destiny or will you make that decision that while you wait on the light to change you will keep the engine of your peace running? Without peace, the stop will become weighty and frustrating. The misunderstanding in the marriage makes it seem unbearable; the sickness tells you that you are going to die but the peace of God tells you that it is not over. In 2 Kings chapter 4, the woman lost her son, his life came to a stop, but she had such peace that she declared, "It is well." While you wait on the change can you declare that it is well? Now is definitely not the time to be consumed with worry and other distractions. While the disciples waited on the promise they prayed, they kept their eyes on the light, they believed the change was coming and surely, they got the divine outpouring.

And suddenly there came a sound from heaven as of a rushing mighty wind, and it filled all the house where they were sitting. And there appeared unto them cloven tongues like as of fire, and it sat upon each of them. And they were all filled with the Holy Ghost and began to speak with other tongues, as the Spirit gave them utterance. (Acts 2:2-4)

There has been a popular misunderstanding of the red light. The red has three meanings, but we only focus on one stop. Stop by itself is final but the second meaning is- pause. Because it is a pause you do not get to shut off the engine and go to the supermarket or the bank. The pause is necessary to allow others to grasp their green. Please understand, your pause activated someone's green. Your pause made room for other persons to enter into their possibilities.

The third meaning of the red light is continuation is in close proximity. Because it is a pause, you must remain in anticipation mode- to go again. Therefore, continue looking out for the follow-up green light. You will never see a red light followed by a yellow light. Whenever you are called to stop/pause do not become discouraged, but rather excited.

There is a certain upgrade, a clearer understanding of the blessing that can only be manifested after you have experienced the red light.

MALFUNCTIONING TRAFFIC LIGHTS

Traffic lights malfunction for many different reasons, power outage, inclement weather or the bulbs in the signal die. In many instances said malfunction causes confusion, longer delays, or even accidents as drivers become unruly. In the same manner, life can be unpredictable, things stop working, friendships start acting up and leave us in a bit of quandary. However, life must go on. The drivers who encounter a broken traffic light simply cannot shut off their engines and walk away from their vehicles. Said drivers must quickly decide that they will approach with caution and pull on the right-of-way rules that provide a safe way to navigate the path. Your marriage, the relationship with your children may have malfunctioned but do not let that deter you. You are still able to defy the odds. In the midst of the malfunction seek the right of way rule in the word of God. Paul says in Philippians 2:3:

"Do nothing out of selfish ambition or empty pride, but in humility consider others more important than yourselves."

Brokenness is a natural part of life. Things go wrong. Our relationships with others will experience power outages, and the light bulbs in the marriage union may have a shortage. However, it is still possible to love and preserve the relationship.

There are provisions made for malfunctioning traffic lights- traffic police. This is where a police officer will direct the flow of traffic until there is restoration. The presence of that officer notifies all road users that there is a problem, but traffic cannot be allowed to stand still. Movements must be continued and subsequently, a temporary solution has been implemented. You too will encounter challenges that are pressing you to stop. Let it be known that, while you wait for the permanent fix, you shall implement temporary solutions and continue the journey of life.

EMERGENCY

The law makes provision for the traffic light signals to be overruled in the event of an emergency. Emergency vehicles like ambulances and fire engines with siren blaring are not subjected to stop at a red light. They must however approach cautiously and proceed when it is safe to do so. Facilitating that safety is the cooperation of the other road users, be it pedestrians or other motorists. Your private vehicle is equipped with a horn and hazard lights which when activated together, shouts an emergency. The same privileges afforded to the ambulance and fire engines are now the private vehicles' favor.

In our lives, we will have emergencies that will require us breaking the standard established protocols. It is dangerous to treat an emergency casual or without the required intensity and intentionality that it demands.

In the account of 2 Kings, the Shunamite woman had an emergency and altered her behavior to match the situation. Her son was dead.

When he had taken him and brought him to his mother, he sat on her knees till noon, and then died. And she went up and laid him on the bed of the man of God, shut the door upon him, and went out. Then she called to her husband, and said, "Please send me one of the young men and one of the donkeys, that I may run to the man of God and come back." So, he said, "Why are you going to him today? It is neither the New Moon nor the Sabbath." And she said, [e]"It is well." Then she saddled a donkey, and said to her servant, "Drive, and go forward; do not slacken the pace for me unless I tell you."

2 Kings 4: 20-24

She knew that what was required was not the norm, but protocols had to be broken. This is where your desperation must be activated against the pull to stop and settle. She rejected the lies of death and pursued the change she desired. What about you, will you pursue victory or accept being stopped at defeat?

GREEN   YELLOW

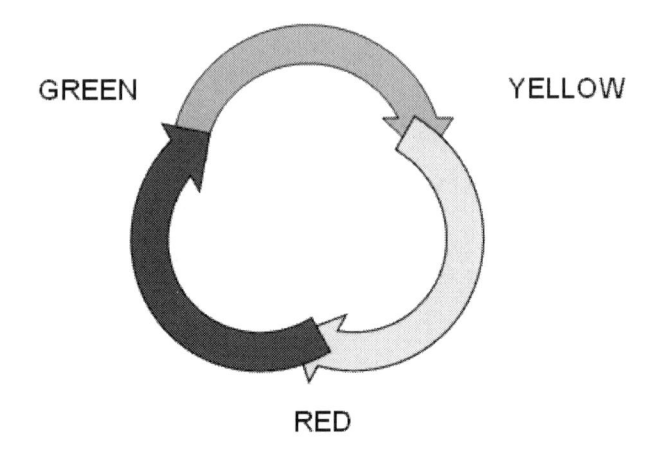

RED

Chapter 2

Fear

I have heard many meanings to the acronym F.E.A.R. but false evidence appearing real is my favourite. The Merriam-Webster dictionary defines fear as an unpleasant, often strong emotion caused by anticipation or awareness of danger. The Greek word for fear is phobos which means to panic. Fear causes you to panic and, in many cases, stops you from pursuing your dreams. In the same manner, the red light brings the traffic to a halt, fear, if left unchecked, can be crippling. However, fear is not of God.

It is a debilitating spirit that must be rebuked. Fear is an enemy and is not of God. Rather than allowing fear to dictate your life, you need to exercise power over fear." Instead of fear, God gave us control "And God said, let us make man in our image, after our likeness: and let them have dominion over the fish of the sea, and over the fowl of the air, and over the cattle, and over all the earth, and over every creeping thing that creepeth upon the earth" (Genesis 1:26).

Therefore, when Satan tries to use fear to block your progress, remind him that God has already given you dominion. It is said that "fear not" or "do not be afraid" is the most repeated command in the Bible. God knew that we would be fearful hence He saw the need to reassure us. In Joshua chapter 1 the children of Israel stood on the brink of the promise. After forty years of wandering, they were ready to enter the Promised Land. However, Moses, the deliverer, was now dead and the formidable city of Jericho was immediately placed before the promise. Yet God said to Joshua, "Have I not commanded you? Be strong and of good courage; do not be afraid, nor be dismayed, for the Lord your God is with you wherever you go" (verse 9). Leading the Israelites into the promise may have seemed like a daunting task but God told Joshua do not let fear drive the wind out of your sail. God knew that a fearful leader was already a defeated leader. A fearful person will never fully walk in and claim the promises of God.

Fear will take your ability to achieve what God has promised. It will paralyze you from starting that business. That book that you need to write, fear will make you believe that you are not smart enough or you do not have the money to publish your work. Fear is like a termite; it eats away your faith and robs you of purpose. The late Myles Munroe said, "Until purpose is discovered, existence has no meaning, for purpose is the source of fulfillment" Fear will cause you to live an unfulfilled life of regret and stagnation.

Fear robs you of the divine. In 2007 at a church service in Jamaica, a powerful worship and prayer session was climbing to a wealthy place. Suddenly, an unexpected silence erupted from her- she saw a lizard. That was it! Her praying and worship came to a crushing halt because of the presence of a lizard. Her fear of lizards was powerful enough to downgrade her from the spirit realm to the physical. The minister leading the service was paralyzed by fear. Fear is so dangerous, if you don't take control of fear, fear will control you. You must fight fervently to retain control of your life.

Where is your focus? Your focus will either give birth to faith or fear. There are persons whose focus has been captivated by presenting giants and the obstacles they might face instead of the grandeur and the promises of their God. Likewise, Peter in Matthew chapter 14:29-30; got the green light to walk on water. Apart from

Jesus, he is the only man who could testify of that favor. Yet during his miraculous walk, fear plucked his eyes off the Master and plunged him into sinking mode.

"So, He said, "Come." And when Peter had come down out of the boat, he walked on the water to go to Jesus. But when he saw that the wind was boisterous, he was afraid; and beginning to sink he cried out, saying, "Lord, save me!"

Fear will never elevate you, do not entertain it or take it for your friend. Bishop Dale Bonner says "Fear engages the principle of magnification; whatever you focus on gets bigger. What you magnify in your mind you magnify in your soul" Begin to shift your focus on the positives and not the negatives, on your strengths and not your weakness, on your blessings and not your wants and needs. When you focus on your blessings you will realize how truly favoured you are. Satan wants to stop you by ensuring that you focus on your lack and shortcomings, but arise, take hold of that greatness within, and march into your promise.

KEYS FOR OVERCOMING FEAR

- Conquer fear through confrontation; meet it head-on. Defeat the fear of failure by trying. Keep going even if you have failed multiple times before. Jimmy Cliff said, "You can get it if you really want but you must try and try, you'll succeed at last." As an inventor, Edison made 1,000 unsuccessful attempts at inventing the light bulb; but guess what, the 1001 attempt he hit the jackpot. Imagine if he had given up? The possibility exists that the light bulb would not have been invented.

- Counteract fear with faith and the word of God. The more you
- Study and implement the word of God in your life daily. This is the strategy of increasing your faith. Let your faith be the handcuffs to fear. Fear must not be allowed to be free to act. The imprisonment of fear must be one of your priorities. God's word repels fear and releases confidence, peace, and hope. The word of God exposes you to the knowledge of God and reminds you of His promise that He is always with you. 1 John 4:18 states there is no fear in love, but perfect love casts out fear. Fear has to do with punishment. However, God's immeasurable love for you surpasses your fears and gives you peace. His love quiets your fears and gives you confidence in Him.

- Attack fear with prayer - Apostle Joshua Selman defines Prayer as "God's authorized system of communion and fellowship with Him". As you commune with God, be bold knowing that you have unlimited access. When fear attacks you, tell God about it. Build an altar of prayer before God trusting and believing that He will help you overcome all your fears.
- Have an intimate relationship with God. You develop a relationship with God by spending time in the word and prayer. God wants to spend time with us. He says in Isaiah Chapter 1, "Come let us reason together."

Mark chapter 6 gives the account of Jesus walking on water towards the disciples during a storm.

"And about the fourth watch of the night he came to them, walking on the sea. He meant to pass by them,

but when they saw him walking on the sea, they thought it was a ghost, and cried out, for they all saw him and were terrified. But immediately he spoke to them and said, "Take heart; it is I. Do not be afraid" (Verses 49-50).

The disciples were afraid, but Jesus' presence calmed their fears and reassured them. When you experience fear do not try to deal with it on your own, call upon Jesus and allow Him to calm your fears. Jesus' presence is the antidote for fear.

Chapter 3

Doubt

What is doubt? The Oxford Languages Dictionary defines doubt as a feeling of uncertainty or lack of conviction. Doubt can also be defined as a lack. of faith. Faith is being sure of what we hope for, certain of what we do not see.

Doubt blinds you. It robs you of your ability to believe that you can do it. It creates an atmosphere of procrastination which leads to non-productivity and time wasted. Many unfulfilled dreams and assignments are buried in the graveyard because their carriers allowed doubt to strip them of their God-given ability to achieve. Do not allow doubt to stop you from fulfilling your purpose or reaching your destiny. As human beings, we love to be in the know.

Therefore, the unknown will tell us to doubt and fear. However, flip the script; confuse those emotions by telling them that you are already a winner. Many patriarchs in the Bible started out as real doubters. When God told Abraham and Sarah, they would be parents, they were already old, as a result Sarah laughed. Gen. 18:12-14

Are you laughing in unbelief at the assignment that you have been given? Do you doubt because you think you are too old to get married, to return to school or to start that business? Well, the Colonel started KFC at age 42, Sam Walton started Walmart at age 44, and Ferdinand began Porsche at age 56, so what is stopping you? When God told Moses to return to Egypt to lead the people of Israel out of slavery, he doubted big time; in fact, he told God he could not speak; Exodus 3: 10-15, 4:10 but look at the mighty deliverance God wrought through Him.

God used Moses, the man who doubted to deliver his people from the brutality of Pharaoh. To eliminate his doubt, God performed three miracles in his presence. One- he saw the bush on fire but not being consumed. Two- His rod became a snake and then converted back to a rod. Three- His hand when put into his bosom became leprous as snow, when the action was repeated, it returned to normalcy. God is equipped with the resources to change your doubt into victory. Trust Him!

You may not see yourself as the most eloquent, but God knows you have a deliver's heart; do not let doubt stop you. A family member, a community, a country is waiting for you to start walking in your God-given calling. Moses was not the only one with excuses. In Judges chapter 6 God told Gideon he would be a judge; however, he responded negatively.

Additionally, Gideon saw himself through the eyes of doubt and unbelief. Nevertheless, where he saw limitation and weakness; God saw a mighty man of Valor. Gideon's doubt blocked him from accepting the word of God. He could not see through his limitations hence he requested a sign from God to confirm His promises.

And Gideon said unto God, "If thou wilt save Israel by mine hand, as thou hast said, Behold, I will put a fleece of wool in the floor; and if the dew be on the fleece only, and it be dry upon all the earth beside, then shall I know that thou wilt save Israel by mine hand, as thou hast said" Vv.36-40

Today, many people are like Gideon; they allow doubt to plague their thoughts and keep them focused on their limitations and weaknesses before they decide to obey God. They simply fail to see how God can use them. As a result, they defer their assignments, dreams, and possibilities because of the doubt that is clouding their minds. Human weakness is not a surprise to God, He is the one that made you (Genesis 1: 27). You can rely on Him and trust His ability to help you in your weakness. He will provide you with strength, courage, and ability where needed. Archbishop William Duncan said, "starve your doubt and feed your faith." Feed your faith with God's word, remain rooted and grounded in Him and doubt will be removed from your life.

A wave of the sea is a proper description of a person who is hampered by unbelief and doubts. A wave of the sea is without rest, unstable, driven by the winds, and capable of great destruction. Being a doubter delays your progress, crushes your ambitions, and prevents you from achieving all that you can. God does not want you to doubt Him. He wants you to trust in Him with all your heart and lean not on your own understanding;

In all your ways acknowledge Him, And He shall direct your paths Proverbs 3:5-6 Ask yourself these questions? Do I believe that God can give me what I am asking of Him? Do I have confidence in His ability to do what I am requiring of Him? Do I believe that He has equipped me with the ability to do what He is asking me to do? If your answer is yes to all these questions, stop allowing doubt to be the barrier to your next.

A quote on quotling.com states, "Whenever you find yourself doubting how far you can go, just remember how far you have come. Remember everything you have faced, all battles you have won, and all the fears you have overcome." Do not forget that "For with GOD NOTHING shall be IMPOSSIBLE" Luke 1: 38

Chapter 4

Discouragement

*I*t is very easy to get discouraged. Said emotion is not a respecter of persons, titles, wealth, or church affiliation. Discouragement can be defined as a loss of confidence or enthusiasm, or dispiritedness. 'Dis' is a Latin prefix meaning "apart," "asunder," "away," "utterly," or having a privative, negative, or reversing force. Discouragement is the opposite of courage. It shows up unannounced and forces its way into your life with a desire to become a resident. In 1 Kings, Elijah was used mightily by God but in a particular season, he got very discouraged. Chapter 19:2-4 states:

We must be careful after a victory- discouragement is still lurking. Please understand that every victory attracts the onslaughts of the enemy. The purpose is to steal the victory you won. Satan is very ambitious and will always desire to rob you of the best you have. The grace of encouragement is priceless.

Elijah the prophet had such an intimate relationship with God that He declared it would not rain for over three years and God honoured his word. Additionally, God used him to bring the Baal prophets to an open shame. However, that did not sit well with Jezebel and as the scripture states she wanted the prophet dead. Shortly thereafter Elijah became so discouraged he desired to die. It does not matter how spiritual or anointed you are, God may have used you to perform many miracles; the possibility of you becoming discouraged is very real. Do not become complacent, working for God will not prevent the enemy from brutally attacking you. If fear or doubt do not work, he will try discouragement, but do not let that puncture your wheel God is greater than every plan of the enemy. Be vigilant when you become fearful and doubtful discouragement is next in line.

Life is filled with challenges, but God knows how to encourage our spirits. Isaiah 41:10 declares, "Fear not, for I am with you; Be not dismayed, for I am your God. I will strengthen you, yes, I will help you, I will uphold you with My righteous right hand". As God said to Isaiah, He is saying to you I am your strength, I am your power, I am your greatness, you can rely on me, I will take care of you. Do not allow the assignment at hand or the challenges that confront you to make you discouraged just trust me. I got you!

Yes, discouragement will come when results are not forthcoming. Seeds are being planted but there is no growth, no fruits are bearing. You are laboring, believing, and trusting God yet no manifestation of what He has promised you. You have prayed, fasted done all that God has asked of you but still nothing to rejoice about only red light. As you await the change, the natural tendency is to become discouraged, to throw in the towel and walk away. However, The Apostle Paul in Galatians 6:9 admonishes "And let us not grow weary while doing good, for in due season we shall reap if we do not lose heart" We cannot lose heart as we journey through our in-between seasons. The in-between season is when the seed has been planted and you are waiting for it to grow and bear fruits. This is the season where you try to "wait without "the weight."

Everything within you may be saying you are the only one experiencing trial but the Pastor or Bishop you see preaching by fire may be walking through his or her season of discouragement as well. Therefore, as you wait do not get frustrated with others. Be intentional, and ask God to help you be that source of inspiration for others. Our challenges should not prevent us from exercising brotherly love. Remember others may be discouraged because of the negative treatment you have constantly projected on them. On the other hand, you may be discouraged because of your state of being. Probably you are disheartened because you are still single; you are tired of being the maid of honor or the best man. While there are persons who are praying to get out of their marriage or to simply see a light at the end of the tunnel. James was excited when God told him to go and study for four years; however, when the money finished, he got discouraged and decided to quit. Thereafter a friend said to him, "When I just met you, you told me, God sent you to study, are you saying that the God who sent you to study is not able to finance your tuition?

Discouragement caused James to question God's ability to provide and also to keep His promises. However, trust the process, God is faithful to complete the work He has started in you. In 1 Samuel 30 King David, and his men were dejected in spirit as they faced the tragedy of losing their families. However, that was not the end of the story. King David got a shocker from his men. Men, whom he had trained and poured into, decided to stone him. Imagine the discouragement that confronted the king. Nevertheless, King David did not retaliate; he chose to encourage himself in the Lord. "And David was greatly distressed; for the people spake of stoning him, because the soul of all the people was grieved, every man for his sons and for his daughters: but David encouraged himself in the Lord his God" verse 6. The king had a choice, and he chose encouragement. He found strength in the Lord. You too can find strength in the Lord. When lies are told against you, when you are rejected or persecuted, the purpose to adopt King David's mindset and turn to God to give you strength to push through and be triumphant in Him. Confuse the enemy with your strength in the Lord.

Remember it is the enemy's job to flood our minds with discouragement. Therefore, if rejection from loved ones does not work, he will show you other people's progress and how your life is a failure. He will even send someone to confirm your feelings but do not believe the lies; he tried the very thing with Nehemiah.

Nehemiah in rebuilding the broken walls and burned gates encountered opposition. They were jeered at and classified as feeble Jews. Their building efforts were ridiculed but they continued to build. In his response to their discouraging words, Nehemiah prayed to God.

Let this be your response when negativity tries to impose on your peace. Nehemiah 4:1-5.

Ridicule can cut deeply leaving you discouraged and in despair. Sanballat and Tobiah used ridicule to try and dissuade the Jews from building the wall. However, Nehemiah never appeased the enemy. He chose to pray instead of arguing and delaying the assignment. The enemy wants to delay or stop the work you are doing. When you are mocked or criticized for doing God's will, refuse to respond in self, go to God in prayer, tell Him about what you are experiencing, and remember His promise that He will be with you. Psalm 118: 14 says "The Lord is my strength and my defense he has become my salvation". This will give you encouragement and strength to carry on.

When discouragement comes knocking it is very important for you to know and stand on the word of God. Proverbs 23:7 states as a man thinks, so is he. Tell yourself you are not what Satan or your peers say, you are who God says you are. Replace all that negative energy from the spirit of discouragement with the Holy Spirit. In 1 Samuel we are introduced to a barren woman called Hannah; she was discouraged, bitter and anxious because she was unable to bear children and she shared her husband with a woman who ridiculed her. Although her husband loved and gave her gifts, he could not solve her problem; she wanted children. However, Hannah did not become discouraged, she channeled her discouragement and grief into prayer.

And she was in bitterness of soul and prayed to the LORD and wept in anguish. 1 Samuel 1: 10

She brought her problem honestly before God and persistently sought his help. You may be facing times of barrenness, at work, church or relationships; all your good work is not bearing fruit and it has become difficult to pray.

However, I encourage you to be like Hannah and discover that prayer opens the way for God to work. Things may seem hopeless, but you have what it takes to

counteract the spirit of discouragement with your praise and thanksgiving unto God. Whether others are jeering you like Nehemiah and Hannah or it is illness, financial struggle, family problems or the other countless things life throws at you; God desires to give you beauty for ashes, the oil of joy for mourning, and the garment of praise for the spirit of heaviness; that you may be called trees of righteousness Isaiah 61:3. Do not stop, press pass discouragement and watch God do the miraculous for you. It's the persistence that breaks the resistance!

Chapter 5

Self-Sabotage

Let us face it, you are not always going to get it right. There are moments when you may experience self-loathing, unrelenting frustration that stems from your own hands. It is in those moments that negative thoughts bombard your mind and try to push you into lockdown mode in an attempt for self to be sabotaged. The word sabotage can be defined as to damage or destroy equipment, weapons, or buildings to prevent the success of an enemy or competitor. Life Coach Lisa Jeffs says, "Self-sabotage is when we actively or passively take steps to prevent ourselves from reaching our goals. This behavior can affect nearly every aspect of our lives, be it a relationship, a career goal, or a personal goal such as weight loss. Although very common, it is an incredibly frustrating behavioral cycle that lowers our self-confidence and leaves us feeling stuck" There are many reasons someone may choose self-sabotaging behavior, but many stem from a lack of belief in oneself. Lack of confidence in yourself can cripple your ability to move forward and as such many dreams have been aborted because of this trait. Hebrews 10:35 declares "Therefore do not throw away your confidence, which has a great reward, for you have need of endurance, so that when you have done the will of God you may receive what is promised." There are times when you begin a task with confidence and exuberance, however, as time passes, and results are not forthcoming your confidence slowly diminishes. Nevertheless, the scripture says do not lose your confidence when things are not going the way you desire, do not sabotage your dreams, and pray that the Lord gives you the endurance to push through and complete. After completion or even during the process, pat yourself on the back for starting, for trying, make note of the errors, learn from them, and try again. This is not the time for pausing, keep going and take control of your mind!

Like every other emotion, self-sabotage begins in the mind. The mind is the engine room- or the power bank for your thoughts. When you begin to think negatively, your thoughts will eventually become your words and your actions. "I cannot do this", "I am not good enough" "I quit" You are only plunging yourself further into defeat. Even now while writing this book so many negative thoughts have inundated my mind. However, I choose to ignore them and continue writing. Granted there were times when I began listening to the voices and stopped writing. Nevertheless, I decided to push on amid the fight. A dear friend of mine once told me "Not every thought must be spoken." The truth behind said advice is that your words have power. Proverbs 18:21 tells us "Death and life are in the power of the tongue, and those who love it will eat its fruits." Your words are figuratively the fruit of your mouth. What type of fruits are you bearing? Are you speaking words of defeat, sabotage, fear, or doubt? or are you speaking or bearing words of empowerment, hope, positivity, life, love, and joy? A witness in a court for example can help determine, by his words, whether a defendant lives or dies. Your words can bring death as well as life.

The enemy attacks you first in your mind. Whoever or whatever controls your mind controls you. One day during devotion a friend messaged me and shared a picture of someone. The individual was someone I wished I were, because of what that person had. As soon as I looked at the picture, I immediately started to think negatively in light of what the picture represented for me. It showed what I was lacking, what my heart desired. I began to focus on what I was missing, and it caused me to become sad. At that moment I no longer wanted to continue my devotion to God. I allowed my thoughts to dictate my actions; sabotage stepped in and robbed me of my time with God. Do not take your thoughts lightly; the mind is literally a battlefield that is where the war begins with you and the enemy. As a child of God, you already have the mind of a winner, therefore, do not succumb to self-sabotage. Feed your mind with the things of God and not the lies of the flesh. Through the word of God, prayer, and fasting you will experience change. The Apostle Paul says "Whatever things are true, whatever things are noble, whatever things are just, whatever things are pure, whatever things are lovely, whatever things are of good report, if there is any virtue and if there is anything praiseworthy—meditate on these things" Philippians 4: 6. Whatever we feed our minds will be seen in our words and actions. Therefore, we must be cognizant of what we allow to enter our thoughts through the books we read, the internet, television shows we watch, and conversations in which we engage. The renewal of the mind is critical. It is a must for us to be fully transformed. A renewed mind will not become a victim of self-sabotage. A renewed mind is focused, alert, determined, engaging, thoughtful, blessed, intentional, prepared, and strong.

Chapter 6

Insecurity

*E*verybody deals with insecurity from time to time. It can appear in all areas of life and come from a variety of causes. It might stem from a traumatic event, patterns of previous experience, social conditioning (learning rules by observing others), or local environments such as school, work, or home.

Insecurity can be defined as a feeling of inadequacy (not being good enough) and uncertainty. It produces anxiety about your goals, relationships, and ability to handle certain situations. It can also stem from general instability. People who experience unpredictable upsets in daily life are more likely to feel insecure about ordinary resources and routines. Some of the more common areas insecurity is manifested are relationship, social, body image, and intellect.

Not having complete confidence in God is a form of insecurity. Insecurity robs you of your true potential and creates a vacuum that can leave you despondent and discouraged. Fear and doubt are forms of insecurity; they consume your being thus cutting off access to God's assistance and guidance. Left unchecked said insecurities can lead you to believe lies about your abilities and also how God can use you to fulfill His purpose. However, when lack of confidence threatens to cloud your mind remember what God says in Psalms 139: 13-14, "For you formed my inward parts; you knitted me together in my mother's womb. I praise you, for I am fearfully and wonderfully made. Wonderful are your works; my soul knows it very well". If you should feel worthless or even begin to hate yourself, please remember that the Holy Spirit is ready and willing to work within you.

It is possible that you may feel insecure about your body's image, your jobs, how others perceive you, your relationship with your spouses, friends, families, and even with God. At times you even question who you are. You belittle your self-worth by comparing yourself to others; eventually, low self-esteem will creep in. Jeremiah the Prophet was mightily used by God, but he too suffered from insecurity. Therefore, God told him,

"Before I formed you in the womb, I knew you…Before you were born, I sanctified you; ordained you a prophet to the nations" Jeremiah 1:5. Jeremiah felt inadequate to be a prophet and did not think that God could use him; however, God saw beyond his insecurities. He served for forty years and continuously warned the Israelites about the Babylonian attack and captivity. The prophet who saw himself as being inferior became a mighty battle axe for God. With this knowledge, we should come to the understanding that there is no need for us to feel inferior, inadequate, or unworthy. Like Jeremiah God knew who we were going to be before we were conceived in our mother's womb. We must not limit our abilities when we have God as our divine helper. Do not fall prey to the wiles of the devil. One of the enemy's tricks is to make us forget who we are in Christ." You are too valuable to God for you to think low of yourself. Like Jeremiah, God can use you to be a positive world changer. Do not underestimate God's ability to use you for His purposes.

As we examine the records of God and Jesus, one cannot miss the similarity of- no insecurity. God never showed any form of insecurity when He spoke and established the universe. Nor did Jesus when He declared He would be risen on the third day from the grave. They were certain that their utterances would be accomplished.

Chapter 7

Procrastination

Procrastination is a powerful weapon used to delay or stop you from achieving your very best. "I will get it done tomorrow, "you tell yourself. Then tomorrow turns into a week later, then a week turns into a month, and a year later you still have not applied for school, write that book, open that business.

The act of unnecessarily postponing decisions or actions is known as procrastination. These actions and decisions can lead to time wasted. One of the leading figures of early American history, Benjamin Franklin is quoted as saying "Lost time is never found again".

The truth is procrastination can be deceptive and sometimes parades as wisdom; one such deception is thinking you have time. Why bother doing it now when I have time to do it later? "Why the haste to serve God now? Why not live my life the way I think is best without being subjected to the will of God?" Broken relationships that need to be mended with great urgency are delayed because of unforgiveness. However, if death comes before reconciliation, then regrets such as I would, I could, I should, are sentiments that may be echoed. Why put off what can be done today for tomorrow? Now is the time to act, now is the time to pursue, and now is the time to conquer. "Make hay while the sun shines" is a well-known saying which shows us the importance of always going amid the odds. Proverbs 10:5 states, "He that gathereth in summer is a wise son: but he that sleepeth in harvest is a son that causeth shame." A hard-working person works when and how they can; the lazy person misses even the obvious opportunities to get ahead and remains in a place of familiarity, indecisiveness, uncertainty, stagnation, and procrastination. The price that you pay for procrastination is the life you could have lived; that is too heavy a price to pay and must be avoided.

In Joshua 18: 3-6, the Israelites experienced a delay in their blessings because of procrastination.

"So, Joshua said to the people of Israel, how long will you put off going in to take possession of the land, which the Lord, the God of your fathers, has given you? Provide three men from each tribe, and I will send them out that they may set out and go up and down the land. They shall write a description of it with a view to their inheritances, and then come to me. They shall divide it into seven portions. Judah shall continue in his territory on the south, and the house of Joseph shall continue in their territory on the north. And you shall describe the land in seven divisions and bring the

description here to me. And I will cast lots for you here before the Lord our God."

Joshua asked why some of the tribes were putting off the job of dividing and possessing the land. Their delay in dividing and fully occupying the land was time wasted and could have given the enemy an opportunity to return. Oftentimes we delay doing things that seem challenging, boring, or disagreeable. To continue putting off those things can be seen as irresponsible, poor stewardship of time, and in some cases, disobedience unto God.

Procrastinating can be costly. A Christian Airline Pilot was prompted by the Holy Spirit to expedite the departure time that resulted in saving over 140 passengers' lives. He instructed his crew to take a shorter, 20-minute break before the plane was due to take off for Jakarta via Ujung Pandang. Only minutes later, a powerful 7.5 magnitude earthquake struck the area resulting in underwater landslides that apparently triggered a massive 10 to 20-foot tsunami that swept through Palu and other coastal areas. At least 1200 people's lives were lost. (www.godreports.com)

Had he procrastinated and not been obedient to the Holy Spirit additional lives could have been lost including his own. Procrastination gives birth to missed opportunities, stagnation, and laziness. It can be extremely detrimental to your ability to productively pursue your goals with success.

Procrastination is a deadly camouflage used by the enemy to restrict your potential and or derail the plans of God.

Your lack of motivation and indecisiveness are two causes of procrastination that can cause you to wait until the ultimate deadline to pursue your goal. In doing so you may not be able to put in your best efforts, and the quality of work might not be the best. Waiting until the last minute to study for an exam or work on a presentation for work can lead to unfavorable results that can be damaging to your achievement.

In late 2019, Covid19 made its debut in North America and led us into a Global Pandemic. One of the lessons we can learn from the pandemic is that life is short and can change in an instant; therefore, every moment must be treasured. As the world came to a halt many of us began to realize time is of the essence and many dreams and aspirations that were placed on hold must now be brought to fruition. All the excuses we had before about not having enough time or being too tired were no longer valid. Many businesses and ministries were birthed in the midst of the pandemic. Talents and skill sets were discovered, and dreams became a reality for many. Oftentimes it takes a tragedy to get us moving as we come to the realization that we don't have all the time in the world as we first thought.

Ask yourself what is stopping you from just doing it.

Chapter 8

People's Opinion

"Your path is unique and special. Just like you! So, checking in with your intuitive knowledge about who you are and what you really desire is essential to let go of others' opinions. Because then you'll always have a connection with your truth" Dr. Ashlee Greer, Social Philosopher. You cannot stop what others say about you, but you can stop and take control of its effects on your life.

You should not allow your self-esteem to be attached to people's opinions. If you allow same to happen, you will always be in a state of uncertainty. The many likes or dislikes you receive on social media should not define who you are. "No one can make you feel inferior without your consent" (Borrowed), do not give others such power over you. Come to the realization that you will never please everyone; therefore, I encourage you to pray, "Lord deliver me from the opinion of others." I am not advocating that you must be arrogant and not listen to or respect the opinions of others, but people's opinions should not hold you captive. Men's opinions should not stop you from fulfilling your purpose. The question was asked, "Why are you so concerned about the opinion of others?" The truth is you matter because people matter. You must coexist on this earth with people. However, you should never allow people's beliefs to dictate your every move or thought process.

The harsh reality is that people's opinions can be damaging. A former prostitute got saved and the Pastor's son fell in love with her. However, the church did not approve of their relationship; they saw her as damaged goods. How people see you is not as important, it is how God sees you, and how you see yourself. Are you seeing yourself through the lenses of persons or through the lenses of God?

Have you elevated a person's opinion of you over God's truth about you? If yes, that can be a major source of discouragement. Nevertheless, said problem can be easily fixed by putting God's truth in its rightful position. The truth about that former prostitute is that she is now the righteousness of God in Christ Jesus (2 Corinthians 5:21). In Christ, she is a new creation, her old has passed away; behold, the new has come. They saw her as damaged goods based on her former life, but the blood of Jesus washed away all her sins and gave her the opportunity to position herself in becoming the Pastor's daughter-in-law. Had the Pastor's son listened to others, He would have allowed their opinion to rob him of God's plan to have a wife with a life changing testimony that can bring others to Christ. Though she was being criticized by some of the females for her former life they could also benefit from her conversion by getting hints about satisfying their husbands thus preventing them from lusting after other women.

You are never so damaged or broken that God cannot fix you. We should never write people off because the God that we serve can turn a Saul into an Apostle Paul (Acts 9:1-19) When God begins to mold and shape you into his image, perfection in Christ is guaranteed. As long as you are a child of God you are never damaged goods. Others may project their opinion because behind the critique they are jealous, jealous of your transformation and your accomplishments. However, let the critique work to your benefit. Rev. Leostone Morrison says' Critic me until I become my best me" (Mind Renewal Biblical Secrets To A Better You).

On the other hand, a friend lost his business, and a dear family member compared him to a friend who was doing well. Not only did he lose his business, but his marriage also ended in divorce, while the friend was doing well in both areas. Fortunately, my friend was not shackled by the opinion of men hence he responded. "Our journeys are different; I will be happy for where he is on his journey." I encourage you to never allow another person's journey to cause you to be discouraged. Your journeys are different. Celebrate other people's victory! God is in the neighborhood, and you are next in line for your miracle.

Do not value human beings' opinions over God's and forfeit his influence over your life. Getting other people's opinions should not be frowned upon; however, you should not allow it to take precedence over God's. Psalm 118:8 tells us "It is better to take refuge in the LORD than to trust in man." Caring about the thoughts of others can stop you from doing God's will. Many dreams have died at the gates of people's opinion while leaving you in disobedience with God. It is better to be in the will of God than in the will of man. Note that sometimes God will require you to do things that look foolish in the eyes of men. Nevertheless, Proverbs 3:5-6 declares, "Trust in the Lord with all thine heart and lean not unto thine own understanding. In all thy ways acknowledge him, and he shall direct thy path." God's opinion overrides the opinion of man. You should never reside at the place of man's opinion. Whether it seems negative or positive remain in the will of God. We see this happening to the young prophet who listened to the voice of an older prophet and as a result, he lost his life; 1 Kings 13:15-24.

Do not allow people's negative words to discourage or take you out of God's will. Their words are not just irrelevant, but they can be unhealthy and deadly. What God says about you is final do not let any other voice supersede God's.

A dear friend of mine said, in high school, one of his teachers told him, "You will not amount to anything". He heard the piercing words that had the potential to massacre his potential and future. He however chose to flip the script and prove her wrong. This meant some immediate necessary changes had to be implemented. He pulled back from idling and utilized his time studying. When his exam results were received, he gladly searched for the negative word-spitting teacher and showed her his passes.

Let not the negative, low opinions about you by humans crush you to failure, but rather propel you to greatness. Your victory rests on the determination and consistency of you refusing to let anything stop you. Be stopped no more!

Chapter 9

Worry

"Be anxious for nothing, but in everything by prayer and supplication, with thanksgiving, let your requests be made known to God" Philippians 4:6 NKJV. The mentioned text is frequently quoted but it is often done without application. The text is transformational, yet many people find it extremely difficult to implement in their daily living. The wealth of the text resides in the simplicity and power embedded in the scripture. Do not worry about anything but pray and ask God humbly and while you are doing that give Him thanks, it means simply that. Rejecting worry is a powerful weapon against the devices of the enemy.

Worrying is a solid demonstration of one's belief system. It must be remembered that our lives are a reflection of the state of our minds. A worried or anxious person exposes the location of the mind. The person's mind has refused to acknowledge God as Omnipotent - All-Powerful, Omniscient- All-Knowing, and Omnipresent All-Present.

Additionally, our reaction to the text has also revealed that maybe we do not trust God as we profess. We tend to put our trust in people rather than God. It is easier for us to first call and tell others about our situation than to take it to God in prayer. Sometimes we go to God as a last resort.

However, let us not ignore a powerful truth in the text, "be anxious for nothing" is not an option or a suggestion, it is a command. God expects us to rest in Him and put off fear, doubt, and anxiety. The Psalmist reminds us to Rest in the Lord and wait patiently for Him.

Do not fret because of him who prospers in his way, because of the man who brings wicked schemes to pass. Psalms 37:7 Every place worth entering has an entrance. Some places have doors, gates, or simply designated spots that facilitate entering. Your life is considered worthy of entering by the kingdom of darkness and one area that opens multiplicities of doors to Satan is worry. Worrying gives access to our minds and bodies. When you allow yourself to be consumed with the situation at hand, it blinds you from discovering the already provided solution God prepared for you. In the end, it results in a significant loss of wealth - you miss the lesson that God is teaching you. Nothing that you have gone through, is going through or will go through must be wasted. There are priceless lessons embedded in every situation that presents itself with the beckoning to worry. Unfortunately, we tend to limit God not realizing that we have been equipped with power from above so worrying, and being doubtful, among other negative feelings become the norm for us.

The book of Mathew gives us an excellent account of Jesus exhorting mankind against the error of worry.

But if God so clothes the grass of the field, which today is alive and tomorrow is thrown into the oven, will he not much more clothe you, O you of little faith? Therefore, do not be anxious, saying, 'What shall we eat?' or 'What shall we drink?' or 'What shall we wear?' For the Gentiles seek after all these things, and your heavenly Father knows that you need them all. But seek first the kingdom of God and his righteousness, and all these things will be added to you. (Matthew 6: 30-32)

If we focus on the magnitude - the "bigness" of our God and not our situations, then there will not be any room to exercise worry. An old song says, "Why worry when you can pray?" "Worrying keeps us from the real challenges God wants us to pursue" (borrowed quote).

Persons who faced challenges without worrying:

Then Jesus returned in the power of the Spirit to Galilee, and news of Him went out through all the surrounding regions. Luke 4:14 NKJV

1. So, this Daniel prospered in the reign of Darius and in the reign of Cyrus the Persian. Daniel 6:28 NKJV

2. Then the king promoted Shadrach, Meshach, and Abed-Nego in the province of Babylon. Daniel 3:30 NKJV

All three accounts have the similarity of extreme pressure, maintaining a relationship with God, and victory. Jesus was tempted by the devil; Daniel was thrown in the lion's den and the three Hebrew boys were cast into a lake of fire. Jesus received power - the Holy Spirit empowered Him, Daniel prospered, and the three boys got promoted. There is no record of anxiety, worry, or fear and the results were magnificent. It is therefore safe to conclude that; every mountain you are climbing or wilderness you are going through is a strategy by God to relocate you to a better place. You will come out better! Stop worrying! Your pain is not wasted unless you allow it to be wasted.

If your days are spent worrying about what is currently happening in the world and in your personal life, you will miss your divine assignment at hand. Worrying fixes nothing! It is the anointing power of the Holy Spirit when you go into prayer, praise, and worship, that breaks the yolk of worry, fear, and lack. Whatever your yolk is today, please note that – Worrying fixes nothing!

Therefore, stop allowing worry to imprison you. Be no longer held captive by anxiety. Let today be known as the day of great escape. Do you believe that God is in control, and nothing happens without His knowledge and permission? If the answer is yes, then why are you worried and not trusting Him? Do you know that you are His child?

"But as many as received him, to them gave he power to become the sons of God, even to them that believe on his name:" (John 1:12).

You are not merely a member of a church; you are a son or a daughter of God. What does that mean?

I am a mother. As the reader you may be a mother or father, and you know that children are parents' responsibility; they do not have to worry about school fees, utility bills, security, transportation, or health care among others. In like manner, as a son or a daughter, God has full or complete responsibility for you. Be it, health care, security, or provision that is not your job. Your job is to trust your Father to supply all your needs according to His riches in glory. Please remember your Father is the King of the entire world, including the Kingdom of Heaven; that makes you a royal citizen. You are royalty. Any King that is not able to adequately provide for its citizens is a failing one. Your God never fails.

What am I saying? Stop worrying. What you are stressing about is not your responsibility, it is God's. Let God be God and we continue being sons and daughters.

Chapter 10

Prayer: The Antidote to Worry

Worry will always fight prayer. Every time worrying comes to invade our minds and space, we should exchange that with prayer. Let prayer be your antidote to worry. When you are going through difficulties, do not miss the call to pray, fast, read the word, and seek God more. If said strategies are implemented, you will come out of your problem or wilderness better than you went in.

Prayer is more than talking; it is touching the heart of God. It is giving a voice to your needs. It is that place where you can let down your hair and be real before the One that can change things. In the place of prayer, you can tell God to strengthen you against anxiety and teach you how to find peace in Him. Fifteen-year-old Neda is an exceptional student, but she struggles with anxiety. However, every time she was faced with a challenge, she found refuge in prayer. Once, she had the mammoth task of leading her band as they went live. As she stood, she felt as though she was about to be crippled by thoughts of whether or not she would err but, at that moment, she whispered a short prayer, and that made all the difference. Prayer is the key that unlocks faith and the power of God in our lives.

Jesus the son of God knew the importance of conversing with His Father. He spent hours seeking more of God hence He was not perturbed when the Scribes and Pharisees accused Him even hours before His gruesome death He was not overcome by anxiety. As Jesus thought about carrying the sins of the world on His shoulders He prayed; He emptied His heart before the Father. You too can find renewed hope in prayer.

All the anxious moments that you may be experiencing will wane at the glory of the Father. The song says, "Oh what peace we often forfeit all because we do not carry everything to God in prayer. God wants to do an exchange; enter into prayer mode, give him your anxieties and He will give you, His peace. God takes great pleasure when we pray Proverbs 15:8.

On the other hand, the devil will do everything in his power to stop your prayers because he knows that effective praying will not only expose his plans but render him powerless in your life. Hence, when it is time to pray, Satan will bombard your mind with varied distractions; fatigue, doubt, worry, and fear just to keep you from praying. He will not relent. If his strategies do not work, he will set up persons to shut down your prayer life. Daniel's prayer was used as a weapon against him but even when he faced death he kept on praying. Anxious moments should never shut down your prayer line; instead, they should bring you to your knees.

The channel of prayer facilitates you casting your pain and sorrows unto God; that is where you get your miracles, deliverance, breakthroughs, and victories. It is in prayer that you build and grow in your relationship with God. Archbishop Duncan says, "Prayer is the place between divinity and humanity; it is what brings the supernatural into the natural for us."

God loves it when His children communicate with Him. He says in Jeremiah 33:3, "Call to me and I will answer you and will tell you great and hidden things that you have not known." Said promises can be likened to a mother saying to her 13-year-old daughter if you keep your room clean, I will allow you extra time on the phone with your friends. The mother should not have to give her an incentive or a promise to keep her room clean; keeping her room clean is what she is supposed to do. However, because her mother wants to inspire or encourage her, she makes an agreement with her.

To further concretize the importance and power of prayer, let us examine the book of Nehemiah. When Nehemiah received disappointing news about the state of Jerusalem's wall, he did not become anxious; he went into fasting and prayer before God. "So it was, when I heard these words, that I sat down and wept, and mourned for many days; I was fasting and praying before the God of heaven" Nehemiah 1:4.

He did not run to earthly help; he went into prayer. He went before God and asked for help. From the very beginning, he included God in his plans and concerns. The book of Nehemiah is an excellent story of how prayer works in successfully accomplishing God's will and purpose.

When Nehemiah got discouraged, he prayed (1:4). When discouragement steps in, look to God.

When seeking direction, he prayed (1:5-11). When You do not know which road to take, trust the father's heart.

When seeking assistance, he prayed (2: 1-5). God will not leave you in the problem, He is the present help in the time of trouble.

When under attack, he prayed (4: 4-5; 9). The Lord shall fight your battles and you shall hold your peace.

When weak and powerless he prayed (6:9). Do not be disheartened, God's strength is made perfect in your weakness.

When joyful, he prayed (12:27; 43). Rejoice in the Lord, His joy brings strength.

Be encouraged to put the word of God into practice. Even if the situation gets worse do not become overwhelmed with worry up on praying without ceasing and do not worry. Tell God what you need and thank Him for all He has done then you will experience His peace, which exceeds anything we can understand. His peace will guard your hearts and minds as you live in Christ Jesus Philippians 4:6-7. Praying with the faith that God will answer your prayer pleases Him.

Chapter 11

Adversity

*M*y God not again? That is the question that often comes after some form of adversity. There is no escaping adversity, it is unavoidable. However, do not allow it to stop you; instead, use it to build your character. Ask yourself this question "Can your character sustain pressure when facing adversity?" In adversity, your character should grow, and the pain should produce expansion.

The children of Israel faced great adversity. Pharoah commanded the taskmasters to withdraw the straw, but the Israelites were still expected to make bricks, they were badly beaten but even as they were mistreated, they continued expanding. In the same vein, the lily is a tender plant; however, it has supernatural strength to push back the soil and live. What is stopping you? The adversity you are now facing is just to strengthen your spiritual and physical muscles, to equip you with the strategies to expand into unchartered waters. In the process of defining an individual, one very telling angle of needful examination is adversity. Therefore, how you handle adversity reflects your level of maturity. Paul in Romans 5:3-5 (N LT) says

We can rejoice, too, when we run into problems and trials, for we know that they help us develop endurance. And endurance develops strength of character, and character strengthens our confident hope of salvation. And this hope will not lead to disappointment. For we know how dearly God loves us because he has given us the Holy Spirit to fill our hearts with his love.

Adversity has the potential to expose the strengths and weaknesses of a person's character.

As a result, God will allow you to confront adversity to test your character; to reveal your shortcomings and the attitude of your heart.

Dr. Charles Stanley, Pastor, of Intouch Ministries writes "Oftentimes God demonstrates His faithfulness in adversity by providing for us what we need to survive. He does not change our painful circumstances; He sustains us through them. Can you trust God to keep you in the place of adversity? Paul admonished believers to always rejoice but in many instances, he was in prison. He experienced much tribulation however, he willingly encouraged the Philippians brethren that even in their time of pain and neglect, they should have a joyful heart. How can you rejoice or encourage someone when you are in pain? Being bombarded with afflictions, sickness, and tragedy- be it manmade or natural disaster, Paul is saying because of the God that we serve and the one that lives inside of us as believers we will overcome. He is not telling us to be happy. He is encouraging us to take our eyes off the problems and rejoice in the Lord. Do not allow your emotions to dedicate your thanksgiving unto God. A heart filled with gratitude demonstrates to heaven its appreciation to God for His love and provision.

Naturally, it may seem silly that you are rejoicing in your time of pain, but you are not walking by sight. You are giving thanks because by faith you know that whatever the Lord is allowing must work together for your good, and for His purpose. God is using life's challenges and Satan's attack to help build your character and also to teach you how to persevere and develop complete trust in Him. In Exodus 16:2-3(NLT) The Israelites started complaining about Moses and Aaron. "If only the Lord had killed us back in Egypt," they moaned. "There we sat around pots filled with meat and ate all the bread we wanted. But now you have brought us into this wilderness to starve us all to death."

The people allowed their spirits to be overwhelmed by adversity and as such they despised their freedom. They could not see the blessing that awaited them. Reject the pull to be like the Israelites whining and complaining under the pressure of adversities, instead focus on God, His power, and the liberty that is found in Him. There is a blessing in focusing on His character, His words, and His promises to you. Pray for the grace to worship and give thanks unto Him during your time of adversities. Resist the temptation of wanting to quit or go back to where God has delivered you, you no longer reside there. No going back to Egypt and eating from the enemy's table. Now is not the time to be looking back. God is allowing you to face this adversity to build your endurance, to test your commitment and to teach your patience. You may feel tired, that is perfectly natural, but remember the joy of the Lord is your strength. He will always provide a route of escape1 Corinthians 10:13. If the pressure is too much for you to bear alone, reach out for help. Call a bother or a sister, you do not have to face adversity alone.

Understand that it was never God's intent for you to endure adversity. Pain and suffering were introduced when Adam and Eve sinned, but God did promise that even in her adversity the woman would bring forth life. The pain that you are experiencing at this present time will push you into birthing your purpose and elevate you to a place in God where you are rooted and grounded. Your mindset will be transformed. You will no longer be restricted by limits, but you will grow. After Eve gave birth to Cain she said, "With the Lord's help, I have produced a man!"

God will help you in your pain to produce, increase, and develop. It is hard to comprehend at times why God would allow you to face adversities. While passing through, you may ask, "Where is God?" "How could He allow this to happen to me?" However, the gold must pass through the fire to be purified, the olive must be crushed to produce oil and the athlete must train hard to perform at optimum. The song says, "Trouble don't last always." Psalms 30: 5 declares that "weeping may endure for a night, but joy comes in the morning light!" Your Pain has an expiration date!

How can one get to that place of always rejoicing in the Lord while going through adversities?

- Be thankful to God. Position your mindset in focusing on your blessings and not your circumstances. The Psalmist writes in Psalm 92 It is good to give thanks to the Lord, and to sing praises to his name, O

Most High; To declare his lovingkindness in the morning, And his faithfulness every night!

- Have an attitude of praise and worship – We praise God because He is great, and He deserves it. Praise refocuses our minds from our problems and shortcomings to God. Praise prepares our hearts to receive God's love and the power of His Holy Spirit. Worship is appreciating God for His nature and worth. Worship should not be relegated to church or when it is convenient to us. We give worship unto God through our obedience and our commitment to Him. Praise and Worship allow us to stay aware of God's presence and leadership in all circumstances and uphold an attitude of serving Him. King David penned the Psalm "I will bless the Lord at all times; His praise shall continually be in my mouth. My soul shall make its boast in the Lord; The humble shall hear of it and be glad. Oh, magnify the Lord with me, and let us exalt His name together." Psalms 34:1-3

The Suffering and chaotic situation that you are presently experiencing cannot be compared to the splendour that lies ahead. Do not allow the pain and adversity to overtake you. This is not the time to stop, to quit, or to pause. It is time to be intentional! It is said that "tough times do not last; only tough people do." As the popular song says, when the going gets tough, the tough get going. When adversity comes to derail you dig deep and push ahead

The well-known story of Job is riddled with adversity, but Job did not give in.

Job 2:10 says, "But he said to her, you speak as one of the foolish women speaks. Shall we indeed accept good from God, and shall we not accept adversity?" In all this Job did not sin with his lips." Job experienced great levels of adversity; he lost all his possessions, and his children (Job 1:13-20) and was afflicted with sickness (Job 2: 7-8) yet Job did not curse or sin against God. The message of Job is that we should not give up on God when He allows us to experience adversity. Yes, God is able to deliver us from suffering, but He may also allow it for reasons we may not understand and also for Him to get the glory.

2 Corinthians 4:16-18 states, "Though our outer self is wasting away, our inner self is being renewed day by day. For this light momentary affliction is preparing for us an eternal weight of glory beyond all comparison, as we look not to the things that are seen but to the things that are unseen. For the things that are seen are transient, but the unseen things are eternal."

Adversity is temporary; it was not sent to break you but to give your faith room to grow in God.

Chapter 12

Sin

*E*instein said insanity is repeating the same thing but expecting a different result. If said quote is true, then it can be deduced that there are many insane persons walking around. What constitutes that madness you may ask? The continued pursuit of sin while expecting a change. Before God created Adam, He being God, provided all that Adam would need to live in comfort. Adam only needed companionship and shortly thereafter that was dealt with. What was given to Adam was a life of perpetual luxury. Today we pursue luxurious living through cars, homes, fancy clothing, expensive perfumes, and others, but there is still a void. Nothing can compare to the love that God gave Adam. God would often meet with Adam and talk with him. Additionally, Adam had the luxury of walking among the lions, tigers, snakes, scorpions, and other animals and insects without fear. Adam lacked nothing. He did not know hunger or thirst. However, shortly after sin happened.

Sin stopped many things for Adam and the human race; one of the most important being perpetual living. Due to sin, death entered our human existence, pain in childbirth, the ease of the land producing was stopped, arduous work began, and man was now living in fear. Purity in knowledge was eroded; for the first time, man understood what it was like to be naked. Shortly after, the first family saw hatred and murder between brothers. Everything was now topsy turvy as the luxurious resort home of the Garden of Eden was taken away from Adam and Eve. Whereas today we use security guards to protect our luxurious properties, the security of an Angel with a flaming sword of fire was placed to stop Adam and Eve from returning to the garden. Sin stopped Adam's luxurious garden living.

In addition, man no longer lived for years on end, life span was now reduced to three scores and ten years. Unfortunately, rather than learning from Adam's error, humanity continues to chase after sin intentionally and aggressively. A few years ago, a young lady received a telephone call. The friend on the line said to her the Lord gave me a message for you, He said, 'Don't do it' and ended the conversation. Sometime later the young lady confessed to her friend that she was about to become sexually involved with a friend that night but when the telephone call came in, she became fearful and did not pursue it. A short time later she found out that the gentleman she was about to become intimate with that night was HIV positive. Sin was presented to her in an attractive package that she desired. Sin desired her death sentence. What is your relationship with sin? Proverbs 1:20 declares "My son though sin entices you consent not." The writer here explains that sin is attractive. The truth is the paintings of sin and the devil looking all crazy and ugly might not be the picture that hell will present to you. Hell may present to you a glorious, wealthy-looking place but none of that is true.

When Satan approached Eve, he showed her why the route of sin should be pursued, he told her God lied, and she would be like God and that made his suggestion attractive. Sin is attractive. Today we continue to chase after sin with all the energy and resources that are available and like Adam and Eve we too have been stopped by that deadly monster.

One of the greatest ways we have been stopped by sin is through our sexuality. The world has been consumed by the perversion of sex, especially that of prostitution which rakes in millions of dollars per year. Unfortunately, some young, misguided girls and boys who use their bodies for financial gain will tell you God told Moses (Exodus 4: 2) to use what he has or Elijah (2 Kings 4) saying to the widow, what do you have in the house? Use it. They have reasoned that God has given them a very attractive body and face; hence they must use said gifts to obtain revenues and survive. This line of reasoning is incorrect. God does not condone sin. Ephesians 5:11 "Take no part in the unfruitful works of darkness, but instead expose them."

Along with sexual perversion, sin also parades itself in the form of jealous rage and murder. In Genesis 4: 8 – Cane became jealous of his brother Abel because God chose to accept his offering and that put Cane in a dark place. Cain spoke to Abel his brother and as they were in the field, Cain rose and killed him thus ending the first sibling relationship. Today that continues with not just siblings but there are awesome relationships that sin has killed. Additionally, it was sin that caused God to destroy the world saving Noah, his family, and the animals (Genesis 6-9).

Sin also makes us crave what is not ours. The story is told of a young man who was raised in a garrison community. He was quite ambitious but lacked the opportunity to excel and make a better life for himself and his family. As a result, he prayed asking God consistently to grant him that opportunity. Finally, the break came, and he received a job at a well-known commercial bank. His family was so proud of him; his peers admired him and wanted to be like him. Every morning he dressed sharp for work. Unfortunately, one day the news came that he was fired from the job and was under investigation for stealing the bank's money. That promising young man's dream was shattered because of the sin of greed. Greed led to stealing, stealing resulted in him losing his dream job and tarnishing his reputation. The investigation resulted in him being charged and was given probation because he had no prior criminal record. A few years later he became addicted to drugs. Although he was a promising young man, he was not able to engage in a meaningful conversation because his words were not cohesive, and his thought pattern was obviously distorted. Sin should not be played with.

Romans 6:23 declares "For the wages of sin is death, but the gift of God is eternal life through Jesus Christ our Lord." This Bible verse remains true. Sin equals death. God equals eternal life. It is not God's desire for you to die in sin. He wants you to reject sin and accept Him, but He cannot force you to choose Him as He already gave you free will. Do not allow sin to stop you! Choose God's way, it may not be easy at times, but it is the best way. It is the way that will guarantee you victory. Refrain from compromising your position in Christ to obtain earthly possessions. They will not last forever and it is not worth it. Your soul is the most valuable thing you have, and Satan will do everything within his power to stop you. Do not allow him to win! Your soul is too precious!

Chapter 13

Just Do it!

*A*bigail graduated from high school with below-average grades. In high school, she struggled with doubt, and procrastination and was always comparing herself with her peers as she thought she was not smart enough. After high school, she and her family migrated to the United States of America for a better life. While living in America Abigail had the desire to attend university but she did not pursue same because of the issues she faced in high school. Sadly, no one in Abigail's immediate family ever attended university and no one in her extended family ever finished. With that knowledge and the issues, she faced, it seemed harder for her to follow her dream of attending University. As the years flew by, the desire diminished. However, one day she was invited to her daughter's school on "Bring Your Parents to School Day" to speak about her current job as an administrator. After the presentation, one of the students asked her the name of the university she attended. To which she responded, "I did not attend University". The student then asked, "Why?" Immediately, she heard herself saying doubt, fear, and not believing she was smart enough. Right there she was forced to confront her fears in front of a class of eighth graders. Fortunately said confrontation propelled her into applying for university. Three months later she was accepted and is currently pursuing her bachelor's degree in communication.

Abigail allowed fear, doubt, insecurity, and self-sabotage to almost stop her from pursuing her dream of attending university. It took an unlikely source, in the form of a class of eighth graders to get her to just do it! How many of you are like Abigail allowing your dreams or purpose to be derailed by your fears and doubts? Do not think for a second that as a child of God, Satan wants you to succeed. His plan is to steal, kill, and destroy (John 10:10). Fear, doubt, discouragement, self-sabotage, insecurity, procrastination, people's opinions, worry, and lack are just a few of the weapons he will use to try and stop you from being great, successful and a person of purpose.

God is a God of completion; He does not do things halfway as Apostle Paul eloquently writes in Philippians 1:6 "Being confident of this very thing, that He who has begun a good work in you will complete it until the day of Jesus Christ."

Sometimes it may be difficult to relate to men and women in the Bible because what they went through happened centuries ago. However, there are many overcomers in our dispensation. Joyce Meyer is a woman of God who did not allow sexual abuse by her father to stop her from becoming a charismatic Christian speaker and author. She experienced a great deal of turmoil in her early life; but rose from them all to build one of the world's largest Christian ministries. In addition, her books have helped millions of people find hope and restoration in Jesus Christ, and her programs commit to redeeming the words of Jesus Christ by helping people to activate them in their lives.

In one of her books she wrote, "As far back as I can remember, I was sexually, mentally, emotionally and verbally abused by my father until I left home at the age of eighteen. He did many terrible things…some of which are too distasteful for me to talk about publicly. But I want to share my testimony because so many people have been hurt, and they need to realize that someone has made it through their struggles so that they can have hope. More than anything, I want you to know and understand that anyone who has been abused can fully recover if they will give their lives completely to Jesus." Joycemeyer.org.

It was not easy for Joyce Meyer but with the help of God, she chose to fight her way through and overcame being sexually abused and all the other challenges that came with it.

Only you can stop you. You may feel as if you are not making any progress and your spiritual and physical lives are at a standstill, it is like you are stuck in a rut. You are lost at sea and land is nowhere in sight. However, do not allow your valley experiences to frustrate you into giving up or stopping. Let me encourage you with the life of another individual who did not allow his failures or setbacks to stop him. "Abraham Lincoln was the sixteenth President of the United States and due to his role as savior of the Union and emancipator of enslaved people, he is regarded as one of America's greatest heroes. His rise from humble beginnings to achieving the highest office in the land is a remarkable story. He experienced quite a few losses in his political career; he failed in business and had a nervous breakdown. It was while growing into manhood that Lincoln received his formal education — an estimated time of eighteen months — a few days or weeks at a time. He decided to become a lawyer, teaching himself the law by reading William Blackstone's Commentaries on the Laws of England. Biography.com

President Lincoln was resolute despite all the challenges that he faced. He was determined not to fail, but to succeed.

God is All-Wise and All Powerful and His will for our lives is perfect. Our limited understanding will not always grasp His actions. God always has a reason for what you are asked to endure. Understand that His silence does not mean He is absent; He is not numb to our suffering. "For My thoughts are not your thoughts, nor are your ways My ways," says the Lord. "For as the heavens are higher than the earth, so are My ways higher than your ways, And My thoughts than your thoughts. Isaiah 55:8-9

Though discouragement, fear, doubt, and all the other characteristics discussed in this book may come upon you at times, be encouraged to know that God will not give up on you. Partner with God and trust Him and His ability. His sufficiency makes up for our insufficiency and in the end, we are drawn closer to Him. When you feel incomplete or distressed by your shortcomings just remember God's promises and provisions. When you push in faith it commands heaven's attention for "a winner never quits, and a quitter never wins". There is always a way. It may not be easy, it may not be convenient, it may not come quickly; but if you will simply keep going, God will help you find a way to just do it!

Remind yourself:

- God loves you. "And so, we know and rely on the love God has for us. God is love. Whoever lives in love lives in God, and God in them" 1 John 4:16.
- He is always with you. "For He Himself has said, I will never leave you nor forsake you" Hebrews 13:5.
- He is your strength. "I will love You, O Lord, my strength. The Lord is my rock and my fortress and my deliverer; My God, my strength, in whom I will trust; My shield and the horn of my salvation, my stronghold" Psalm 18: 1.
- He has given you the tools to fight against the enemy. "The Armour of God, the Waistband of Truth, The Breastplate of

Righteousness, The Shoes of the Gospel of Peace, The Shield of Faith, The Helmet of Salvation, The Sword of the Spirit, The Word of God" Ephesians 6:14-17.

LET US PRAY:

Father, help me not allow all the characteristics discussed in this book to stop me from fulfilling my purpose, my destiny that was ordained by you. I thank you for granting me the grace to fight and push ahead despite all the challenges I may face. Thank you, Lord, that I am a conqueror, I am an overcomer, and I can do all things to Christ who strengthens me. Amen

Reference

Living with anxiety and finding peace in prayer – Neda's story https://innovista.org/2018/06/anxiety-and-prayer-nedas-story/

About The Author

Hillary Dunkley-Campbell is an ambassador for Christ. She is very passionate about prayer, doing the work of God and truly loves to encourage and empower others. She is currently pursuing her bachelor's degree in Business Administration and Biblical Studies at Tyndale University in Toronto, Canada. She is married and is the mother to three children. "What Is Stopping You?" is her second book.

Made in the USA
Columbia, SC
21 August 2024